A BED FOR THE WINTER

Produced for DK by WonderLab Group LLC
Jennifer Emmett, Erica Green, Kate Hale, *Founders*

Editor Maya Myers; **Photography Editor** Kelley Miller; **Managing Editor** Rachel Houghton;
Designers Project Design Company; **Researcher** Michelle Harris; **Copy Editor** Lori Merritt;
Indexer Connie Binder; **Proofreader** Susan K. Hom; **Series Reading Specialist** Dr. Jennifer Albro

First American Edition, 2025
Published in the United States by DK Publishing, a division of Penguin Random House LLC
1745 Broadway, 20th Floor, New York, NY 10019

25 26 27 28 29 10 9 8 7 6 5 4 3 2 1
001-349664-Nov/2025

Published in Great Britain by Dorling Kindersley Limited

HC ISBN: 979-8-2171-2550-0
PB ISBN: 979-8-2171-2549-4

DK books are available at special discounts when purchased in bulk for sales promotions, premiums, fund-raising, or educational use.
For details, contact:
DK Publishing Special Markets, 1745 Broadway, 20th Floor, New York, NY 10019
SpecialSales@dk.com

Printed and bound in China

Super Readers Lexile® levels BR40L to 300L

The publisher would like to thank the following for their kind permission to reproduce their images:
a=above; c=center; b=below; l=left; r=right; t=top; b/g=background
123RF.com: Manachai Phongruchiraphan / Darkkong 20br, Michal Kadleček / Majk76 6-7, Tawatchai Prakobkit / Prakobkit 19cb, Taina Sohlman / Taina 7bc; **Adobe Stock:** Max5128 3; **Alamy Stock Photo:** imageBROKER.com / Dieter Hopf 16-17, Nature Picture Library / Cyril Ruoso 12bc, Tom Stack & Assoc. / Robert S. Michelson 20-21; **Ardea:** Sven-Erik Arndt 15cb, M. Watson 11bl; Dreamstime.com: Anagram1 17bl, Volodymyr Byrdyak 8br, 23tl, Chris Cornish 12-13, Erin Donalson 9bc, Claudia Evans 21br, Irina Evstafyeva 10-11, Izanbar 22br, 23clb, Sergey Kichigin / Kichigin 6cb, 6br, Kmitu 11br, Ksushsh 10bc, Brian Kushner 18-19, Lucaar 16br; Getty Images: Moment / Saurabh Raj Sharan Photography 8cb, The Image Bank / McDonald Wildlife Photography Inc. 15bl; **Getty Images / iStock:** Callingcurlew23 23cla, E+ / DieterMeyrl 13bc, JacobH 22, Miralex 6bc, 23bl; **naturepl.com:** Edwin Giesbers 4-5, Klein & Hubert 19bl, George McCarthy 1, Bruce Thomson 17br, Gerrit Vyn 14br, 14-15; **Shutterstock.com:** Anna Barv 9bl, Chris Watson 8-9, Zsolyomi 13cb

Cover images: *Front:* **Dreamstime.com:** Oleksandra Klestova (Backgrond), Volodymyr Voronov; **Shutterstock.com:** Look_Studio br; *Back:* **Dreamstime.com:** Irella11 clb, Orensila cr

www.dk.com

MIX
Paper | Supporting responsible forestry
FSC™ C018179
www.fsc.org

This book was made with Forest Stewardship Council™ certified paper – one small step in DK's commitment to a sustainable future.
Learn more at www.dk.com/uk/information/sustainability

Pre-level

A BED FOR THE WINTER

Ruth A. Musgrave

DK

hamster

Winter is coming.
The air turns cold.
Some animals must
get ready.
They will hibernate.
They will sleep
all winter.

Winter is coming.
Time to eat.
This animal eats
and eats.

winter

It gets bigger
and bigger.
The fat keeps it warm
while it sleeps.

grizzly bear

Winter is coming.
The leaves turn brown.
They start to fall.
This animal digs a den.
It will sleep here
all winter.

den

echidna

Winter is coming.
The days get shorter.
Time to save food.
This animal hides
food in its den.
It will have a snack
if it wakes up.

food

chipmunk

Winter is close.
Snow will be here soon.
Time to make a bed.

bed

This animal makes a bed with leaves. The soft bed will keep it warm.

Winter is here!
Time to go to sleep.
These bats stay
in caves.
They hang while
they sleep.
They will sleep
all winter.

cave

bat

Winter is here.
Time to get warm.
This family snuggles.

family

They keep each other warm while they sleep.

Winter is still here.
Time to warm up.
This animal wakes up.

groundhog

nest

It moves a bit
to get warm.
It is still cold
in this nest.
It finds a warmer nest.
Back to sleep!

Winter will end soon.
The sun stays
up longer.
It is a little warmer.
It is almost time
to wake up.
Snore on, bear!

sun

black bears

Winter is over.
It is warm and sunny.
New leaves grow.
Time to wake up.
Spring is here!

Glossary

den
a home an animal digs or makes in a cave

hibernate
to sleep through the winter

nest
a home an animal makes

spring
the season when it gets warmer and plants grow

winter
the cold season when some animals hibernate

Quiz

Answer the questions to see what you have learned. Check your answers with an adult.

1. In which season does it get the coldest?
2. Which animals hang while they sleep?
3. True or False: Some animals make their bed with leaves.
4. Where do some animals sleep in the winter?
5. Which season comes after winter?

1. Winter 2. Bats 3. True 4. Den, nest, cave 5. Spring